Ten Poems from Wales

Fourteen Centuries of Verse

Mae'r llyfr hwn
yn perthyn i

With love
from

Helen x x

Candlestick Press

Published by:
Candlestick Press,
Diversity House, 72 Nottingham Road,
Arnold, Nottingham NG5 6LF
www.candlestickpress.co.uk

Design, typesetting, print and production by Diversity Creative
Marketing Solutions Ltd., www.diversitymarketing.co.uk

Introduction and selection of poems © Gillian Clarke, 2013

Cover illustration © Ian Phillips. *Light on Llyn Ogwen, Snowdonia
2011.* www.reliefprint.co.uk. Ian Phillips is an artist and linocut
printmaker, who lives and works in Mid Wales.

© Candlestick Press, 2013
Reprinted 2015

ISBN: 978 1 907598 16 6

Acknowledgements:
The publisher thanks Gillian Clarke for her generosity and her poem,
'Waves', published here for the first time. Thanks are also due to
Samantha Wynne Rhydderch for 'Dressmaking' which first appeared
in *Agenda* 45.4-46.1and to Paul Henry for 'Segovia Moon', published
here for the first time. We are indebted to the late Anthony Conran for
permission to reprint his translations of 'Song to a Child'and 'The Shirt
of a Lad'; to Robert Minhinnick and Carcanet Press for permission
to reprint 'The Dolphin' from *King Driftwood*, Carcanet Press, 2008.
Dylan Thomas, 'Fern Hill' (*The Poems*, Orion) is used with the
permission of David Higham Associates; our thanks to Bloodaxe Books
and Gillian Clarke for permission to reprint Gillian Clarke's translation
of Hedd Wyn, 'Rhyfel', a version of which appears in *The Bloodaxe
Book of Modern Welsh Poetry*, 2003. 'Sunbright' by Dr Dannie Abse
from *In Extra Time* published by Enitharmon Press (Copyright ©Dr
Dannie Abse 2012) is reproduced by permission of United Agents LLP
(www.unitedagents.co.uk) on behalf of Dr Dannie Abse. Our thanks
to the Alun Lewis Estate and Seren Books for permission to reprint
'In Hospital, Poona (I)' from *Collected Poems* (Seren, 2007) and to
Bloodaxe Books for permission to reprint 'The Cat and the Sea' by
R. S. Thomas from *Selected Poems 1946-1968* (Bloodaxe Books, 1986).

Where poets are no longer living, their dates are given.

Introduction

I was young and dreaming of being a writer when I came across
my first poem by a Welsh poet, perhaps the first contemporary
poem to capture my imagination. It was 'The Cat and the Sea'
by R.S. Thomas, among the great poets of the twentieth century.
The poem caught me and never let me go, and I return to it again
and again, wondering at its simplicity, the trick that makes a cat
sing like the sea, the sea purr like a cat, that stare of gorse. It
changed poetry and it changed the sea. I could have chosen so
many of his poems, too many to leave any out, so I here return to
my first.

The work of R.S. Thomas, collected and read as it appeared, led
me onward and outward to contemporary poetry, as well as back
to the roots of British poetry in the work of Taliesin and Aneirin,
the earliest British poets whose names we know. They wrote, or
sang, in the British (Welsh) language in the bardic traditions of
the sixth century. This tiny sample of ten poems ranges from the
seventh to the twenty-first centuries, merely a taste of an ancient
and continuing literature. The oldest is an anonymous poem
found copied by a scribe in a mediaeval manuscript. English
poetry, especially by those who know or are aware of Welsh,
is haunted by this tradition, and many modern poets writing
in English, from Gerard Manley Hopkins, Dylan Thomas, Ted
Hughes, to Carol Ann Duffy, have been fascinated by its intricate
alliterative pattern and sound, and acknowledge its influence.

Gillian Clarke

The Cat and the Sea

It is a matter of a black cat
On a bare cliff top in March
Whose eyes anticipate
The gorse petals;

The formal equation of
A domestic purr
With the cold interiors
Of the sea's mirror.

R.S. Thomas (1913 – 2000)

Song to a Child

Dinogad's smock is pied, pied –
Made it out of marten hide.
Whit, whit, whistle along,
Eight slaves with you sing the song.

When your dad went to hunt,
Spear on his shoulder, cudgel in hand,
He called his quick dogs, 'Giff, you wretch,
Gaff, catch her, catch her, fetch, fetch!'

From a coracle he'd spear
Fish as a lion strikes a deer.
When your dad went to the crag
He brought down roebuck, boar and stag,
Speckled grouse from the mountain tall,
Fish from Derwent waterfall.

Whatever your dad found with his spear,
Boar or wild cat, fox or deer,
Unless it flew, would never get clear.

Anonymous, seventh-century Welsh,
translated by Anthony Conran (1931 – 2013)

The Shirt of a Lad

As I did the washing one day
Under the bridge at Aberteifi,
And a golden stick to drub it,
And my sweetheart's shirt beneath it –
A knight came by upon a charger,
Proud and swift and broad of shoulder,
And he asked if I would sell
The shirt of the lad that I loved well.

No, I said, I will not trade –
Not if a hundred pounds were paid;
Not if two hillsides I could keep
Full with wethers and white sheep;
Not if two fields were in the bargain;
Not if the herbs of all Llanddewi,
Trodden and pressed, were offered to me –
Not for the likes of that, I'd sell
The shirt of the lad that I love well.

Anonymous, sixteenth-century Welsh,
translated by Anthony Conran (1931 – 2013)

Rhyfel

Gwae fi fy myw mewn oes mor ddreng,
A Duw ar drai ar orwel pell;
O'i ôl mae dyn, yn deyrn a gwreng,
Yn codi ei awdurdod hell.

Pan deimlodd fyned ymaith Dduw
Cyfododd gledd i ladd ei frawd;
Mae sŵn yr ymladd ar ein clyw,
A'i gysgod ar fythynnod tlawd.

Mae'r hen delynau genid gynt
Ynghrog ar gangau'r helyg draw,
A gwaedd y bechgyn lond y gwynt,
A'u gwaed yn gymysg efo'r glaw.

Hedd Wyn (1887 – 1917)

War

Bitter to live in times like these.
While God declines beyond the seas;
Instead, man, king or peasantry,
Raises his gross authority.

When he thinks God has gone away
Man takes up his sword to slay
His brother; we can hear death's roar.
It shadows the hovels of the poor.

Like the old songs they left behind,
We hung our harps in the willows again.
Ballads of boys blow on the wind,
Their blood is mingled with the rain.

Translated by Gillian Clarke

Fern Hill

Now as I was young and easy under the apple boughs
About the lilting house and happy as the grass was green,
    The night above the dingle starry,
        Time let me hail and climb
    Golden in the heydays of his eyes,
And honoured among wagons I was prince of the apple towns
And once below a time I lordly had the trees and leaves
        Trail with daisies and barley
    Down the rivers of the windfall light.

And as I was green and carefree, famous among the barns
About the happy yard and singing as the farm was home,
    In the sun that is young once only,
        Time let me play and be
    Golden in the mercy of his means,
And green and golden I was huntsman and herdsman, the calves
Sang to my horn, the foxes on the hills barked clear and cold,
        And the sabbath rang slowly
    In the pebbles of the holy streams.

All the sun long it was running, it was lovely, the hay
Fields high as the house, the tunes from the chimneys, it was air
    And playing, lovely and watery
        And fire green as grass.
    And nightly under the simple stars
As I rode to sleep the owls were bearing the farm away,
All the moon long I heard, blessed among stables, the nightjars
        Flying with the ricks, and the horses
            Flashing into the dark.

And then to awake, and the farm, like a wanderer white
With the dew, come back, the cock on his shoulder: it was all
    Shining, it was Adam and maiden,
        The sky gathered again
    And the sun grew round that very day.
So it must have been after the birth of the simple light
In the first, spinning place, the spellbound horses walking warm
    Out of the whinnying green stable
        On to the fields of praise.

And honoured among foxes and pheasants by the gay house
Under the new made clouds and happy as the heart was long,
    In the sun born over and over,
        I ran my heedless ways,
    My wishes raced through the house high hay
And nothing I cared, at my sky blue trades, that time allows
In all his tuneful turning so few and such morning songs
    Before the children green and golden
        Follow him out of grace,

Nothing I cared, in the lamb white days, that time would take me
Up to the swallow thronged loft by the shadow of my hand,
    In the moon that is always rising,
        Nor that riding to sleep
    I should hear him fly with the high fields
And wake to the farm forever fled from the childless land.
Oh as I was young and easy in the mercy of his means,
        Time held me green and dying
    Though I sang in my chains like the sea.

Dylan Thomas (1914 – 1953)

In Hospital, Poona (I)

Last night I did not fight for sleep
But lay awake from midnight while the world
Turned its slow features to the moving deep
Of darkness, till I knew that you were furled,

Beloved, in the same dark watch as I.
And sixty degrees of longitude beside
Vanished as though a swan in ecstasy
Had spanned the distance from your sleeping side.

And like to swan or moon the whole of Wales
Glided within the parish of my care:
I saw the green tide leap on Cardigan,
Your red yacht riding like a legend there.

And the great mountains Dafydd and Llewelyn,
Plynlimmon, Cader Idris and Eryri
Threshing the darkness back from head and fin,
And also the small nameless mining valley

Whose slopes are scratched with streets and
        sprawling graves
Dark in the lap of firwoods and great boulders
Where you lay waiting, listening to the waves —
My hot hands touched your white despondent shoulders

— And then ten thousand miles of daylight grew
Between us, and I heard the wild daws crake
In India's starving throat; whereat I knew
That Time upon the heart can break
But love survives the venom of the snake.

Alun Lewis (1915 – 1944)

Sunbright

Sunbright sunbright, you said,
the first time we met in Venice
you, so alive with human light
I was dazzled black;
– like heavy morning curtains
in a sleeping bedroom
suddenly pulled back.

And the first time you undressed,
once more, I, frail-eyed,
undeservedly blessed,
as if it were a holy day,
as if it were yuletide,
and feeling a little drunk,
simply had to look away.

Well, circumspect Henry James
couldn't write *The Turn of the Screw*
till he turned his back on sunbright.
Chair around, just so,
to what was alive, beguiling,
in the Canaletto scene below.

Sweet, all this is true or virtually true.
It's only a poetry-licensed lie
when I rhyme and cheat and wink
and swear I almost need to wear
(muses help me, cross my heart) sunglasses
each time I think of you.

Dannie Abse (1923 – 2014)

Waves

When long ago my father cast his spell
with wires and microphones, he told me
he could send sound on waves the speed of light
to touch the ionosphere -
                        and fall, returning
home to the wireless on our windowsill.

Sometimes now, radio on, half listening, struck still
by a line of verse, a voice, a chord, cadenza,
I remember living light in a breaking wave,
not breath, not fire, not water, but alive,
the sudden silver of a turning shoal,

and I still see words on the radio as fish
or birds homing to earth with their message
                        to settle on the hush
of long waves on a beach in Pembrokeshire,
a staircase in the sea, or in the air,
and skies that hum with murmurations of words.

Gillian Clarke

The Dolphin

It's not the shadow of a cloud or the shape of a shoal
so I ask what's out there –
as if the answer was concealed within myself.

Yes I ask myself what it might be
and after a while it is the swimmer that replies,
daring to show its deft muscle and delphic arc.

Next I start counting with my own heartbeat
and I discover that every ten seconds this swimmer surfaces
like a bowsaw against the sea's green grain,
and that every ten seconds it leaps eastward
off the rocks of Gyrn y Locs towards the Irongate.

There are fathoms between us
but we are familiars. I am sure of that.
Because I have walked where it dives now
and I have swum where it is swimming
through the grey wall slow to fall in rubble,
through the white wall it has mined yet flies above.

And every ten seconds this dark dauphin
of the gwters and the gwlis and the grykes,
every ten seconds the Gulf Stream leopard
hurtles out of the salt thickets
and from where I stand on the cliff's dais
I can feel it coming, I can feel it coming,
so that the sea is changed and will never be the same.

Because here is the oracle of an ordinary tide –
something that cuts a crescent like the dark of the moon.
Then exultant in the air we both must breathe
is the polished ferrule of the dolphin's face.

Robert Minhinnick

Segovia Moon

The moon's a guitar.
It hangs in a tilted sky,
strumming the tides in and out.

Couples stare up and listen
for the promised chord.

Night after night they return
for what their parents heard
or said they heard.

To think, a man's fingers
danced on that grain!

A boy looks for a face,
taps his feet, without knowing
without knowing

under the guitar's moon.

A cow jumps over a guitar.
A violin meows.

A wide-eyed doll
cups her ear
in a blue bay window.

Listen ...

        a bright guitar

pauses on the wires of song.

Paul Henry

Dressmaking

i.m. Maggie Tŷ Cwm c.1920

They might have thought she was dead,
the sailors, as they docked opposite her door,
as if some trick of the light

would dupe them into seeing her propped
in a black box by the stove, but truly she'd be
dictating stitches whilst they crossed

the quay tilting cheap coffins and tea chests
onto the waiting carts. The date of her daughter's
birth was the last thing she'd written

in thread, an epitaph before paralysis
struck. *Cut it on the bias* she'd call,
tack it back as the little girl's fingers

clipped the fabric, felt it fall to a floor
numb with her mother's sprinkled pins.

Samantha Wynne Rhydderch